Parler à Voir

or

Everyone Seems to Be Into Dialogue These Days

by

orde

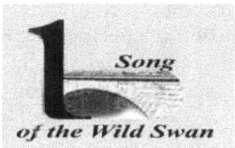

Published by Song, 2014.
Song is an Imprint of:
Song of the Wild Swan Ltd.
1 Folly Bridge, Oxford, OX1 4LB, UK.
www.songwildswan.com
tel +44 (0) 1865 240572
fax +44 (0) 1865 246565
e: info@songwildswan.com

Parler à Voir or
Everyone Seems to Be Into Dialogue These Days by orde
ISBN 9781909777156

First published: *c.* 1980's (Private, 6 copies).
eBook: 2014 Song, Oxford.

Acknowledgements

Song eBook Design series by Laurence Hutton-Smith.
Cover Design: Laurence Hutton-Smith.
Cover Image: *frank,* Oxford (July 2014)
Oil on canvas 45.5 x 35.5 cm, by orde
Extracts: Lyrics on pages 9, 53 and 98 from *The Wall*, Pink Floyd
Book Production: Amaury Marinho Junior.

Contents

Parler à Voir

or

Everyone seems to be into dialogue these days

Key to notation used.

1.		increase voice level
2.		decrease voice level
3.		tone oscillation on word/s, letter/s below this sign
4.		overlap on this on word/s, letter/s below this sign with that of the following speaker's first word
5.		murmur at various pitches - length of murmur indicated as to words or sentences by left stem and the number of words or sentences by the right stem
6.		mumble at various pitches
7.		whisper at various pitches
8.		begin fading of voice
9.1	∧	strongly accent letter, word , syllable or gesture
9.2	>	accent letter, word, syllable or gesture
9.3	—	accent a little the letter, word, syllable or gesture
9.4	⌣	very softly accent the letter, word, syllable or gesture
10.		flutter on letter or word above this sign
11.1	(rX)	speed of words in brackets follow rapidly
11.2	(s)( )	speed of words in brackets follow slowly

12.1	ŏ ⟶ v	Sonorisation : vibrate vocal chords to cause originally voiceless sounds to become voiced
12.2	v ⟶ ŏ	Desonorisation : the voice to fade out of a voiced sound
13.	+	the word below this sign begins on the breath
14.1	▭▷	inhale
14.2	◁▭	exhale
15.	Ϟ	Vetor Click : clicking sound with tongue
16.	▦	sniffs
17.	▲	laughs
18.	▼	sighs
19.	—⊙—	suck in breath
20.1	⊡	very short pause
20.2	∘	pause
20.3	⊙	long pause
20.4	◎	very long pause
21.	↯	Entry sign : vocalisation of next word begins at this point
22.	↯	Cessation sign : vocalisation of word ceases entirely at this point
23.1	⏜ T	telephone rings : short duration
23.2	～ T ～	telephone rings : long duration
24.1	sss (T)	utilisation of telephone
24.2	sss (T) rep	replacement of telephone
25.1	sss T rep	sound of telephone answering machine being played

25.2	$sss\ \overline{\ \ J\ }\ rew$	sound of telephone answering machine being rewound
26.1	$\boxed{I}$	indistinct sounds to be heard
26.2	$\Box$	fade away indistinct sounds
27.1	$\boxed{I^m}$	indistinct music sounds to be heard
27.2	$\boxed{m}$	fade away music sounds
27.3	$\boxed{^m_C}$	music becomes clear and distinct ; no other sounds
27.4	$\boxed{m^m}$	music continues with instrumentation only and ceases completely before vocal entry
28.1	$\curvearrowright^g$	greatest degree of decrease in voice ($\frac{1}{2}$)
28.2	$\curvearrowright^g$	greatest degree of increase in voice (2)
28.3	$\curvearrowright^s$	smallest degree of increase in voice (2:3)
28.4	$\curvearrowright^s$	smallest degree of decrease in voice (1:2)
29.	$\sim B \sim$	sound of breaking bottles
30.1	$\mathcal{R}$	speaker stands
30.2	$\mathcal{R} \rightarrow$	speaker walks
30.3	$\mathcal{L}$	speaker sits
30.4	$\mathcal{L} \rightarrow$	speaker while sitting moves
31.	$\Big\{\ \cdots$	words said or sounds made are said or made in unison

All music used was from the L.P. "The Wall" by Pink Floyd ; Columbia Records.

Parler à Voir

or

Everyone seems to be into dialogue these days

I've got a little black box with my poems in

I've got a bag with a toothbrush and a comb in

When I'm good dog they sometimes throw me a
                                          bone   in

I've got elastic bands keeping my shoes on

got these swollen hands blues

got thirteen channels of shit on the T.V. to
                                      choose   from

I've got electric light

And I've got second sight

I've got amazing powers of observation

I :   sorry   I   what   •   failure is   •   is

meant to be

Y :

I : were you thinking of leaving

Y : yeah

I : why

Y :   whereas   because I am lost

I : you are very very lost and very very stupid too actually

Y : actually yes probably I am but

I : cause I could have said to you get the hell out

Y : why didn't you

I : cause I am not stupid

⊙

Y : oh yeah

I : why did you want to leave • cause I am getting too

• close

•

Y : too close how

•

I : I don't mean physically

Y : ▓

I : was I getting too close to what you are

•

Y : and what am I

I : yea was I • yea was I getting too close to what you are

Y : ⌐and what am I • I am in a difficult situation here

really

I : do you think that I was getting too close to you you said yes

•

Y : yes I I

I : I did not throw you out because I am not • because • I am

sincere • you have a friend in me

Y :(r)(what did you say)what did you say I've a I've

I : I did not throw you out • or I did not say I care or

fuck off or take your bags and go ⊙ so I am

sincere because I understand • and I give you three

chances you have used one

Y : three chances that's

I : I know what I am doing

Y : why what • what is in me • gives you three chances
    why of what

I : because you are desperate

Y : desperate at finding what

I : I don't know

Y : what is the necessitation of sitting down on on a blanket
    and ┼┼┼┼ • where is the • what you know

I : you know what

Y : no its nothing

I : ſno³ what

Y : its not you • maybe its • me

I : sorry

Y : ▼ maybe its a failure I've found • finally

I : maybe its a failure what

Y : I said maybe its a failure of mine Ʉ • why did
    you close the curtains what

I : do you want me to open them

Y : no no I don't give a damn what you do with the curtains
    its your apartment

I : the light is actually brighter now

Y : oh oh bright • why did you close the curtains in the
    first place • getting back to the question of motivation
    again my stupidity

I : not your stupidity so much as your • crass stupidity

Y : feelings

I : what feelings

Y : in a sense I

I : insulting behaviour maybe

Y : pardon

I : insulting behaviour

Y : insulting

I : yes

Y : in what way

I : ascribing   to me   certain things

Y : yeah obviously yeah well yeah

I : and simply because I closed the curtains

Y : yeah that is   very

I :   you ascribe the basest of motives to me

Y : and what motives do you ascribe to yourself

I : not important   you asked me to help you   which you

Y : help me help me what

I : you cancelled out

Y : help me I cancelled out yes many things but

I : No you cancelled out asking me

Y : (s)(a quest of methodology)

I : I said to you I don't know   all I know is that you were
    not being honest with me   yes you were being honest
    you actually did want me to help you but you were not
    prepared to accept any consequence of it that help or
    any attempt of it   you ascribe base motives of
    closing the curtains   that is all you see then

you immediately want to leave Ø   walk right out • you
can   •   anytime

Y : yes Ø (⌐)(there's still no motive in you)

I : pardon

Y :(⌐)(there's still no motive in you)

I : what do you mean there is still no motive in me I want
    to help you the best I possibly can I am not sure how
    or why

Y : yeah I ah and that projects upon me

I : ⌐ ⁀why

Y : ⌐ ··I | I | ☐ ᵥ ⟶ ⌄ₒ

    and I'm not sure I know why

I : you want to know why •   or how

Y : Yeah

I : why •   because you need help

Y : yes maybe I am needing help one needs help in many ways

I : of course you do I could go a further step   •   and
    I could say to you if you want help which you have said
    yes which you have cancelled out and I can ask that
    question again •   and at ⊡ some point I may not ask
    it •   and that is that •   you can always ask for
    help and I can always reject •   I can say I am not
    prepared to   •   to have motives ascribed to me like
    that •   I am not prepared to help you •   anymore
    its my choice •   find your own way if you can •   if
    you can't too bad

Y : yes

I : I can go a step further that that and I can say •   I
    don't want you to question my motives

Y : why shouldn't I question your motives

I : my motives are irrelevant

Y : why are they irrelevant

I : what is the relevance of my motives

Y : what is not the relevancy of your motives

I : if I am what is not the relevancy if I am moving in the right direction my motives are irrelevant   if I am moving in the right direction

Y : yes you ascribe those right directions as your own projections of what is right

I : correct   correct that is all it can be

Y : yes ⊘ maybe I am disillusioned maybe I am lost but that does not neccessitate that that is the right direction of mine

I : correct correct it is only my interpretation or my view as to what can help you at this particular point

Y : at this particular point ☐ what can help me at this particular point

I : what can help you

Y : yes

I : are you asking

Y : ⌠yes

I : you don't know

Y : I don't know many things there's an awful lot that I don't know

I : why did you reject holding hands by the way

Y : why would —•— want holding hands

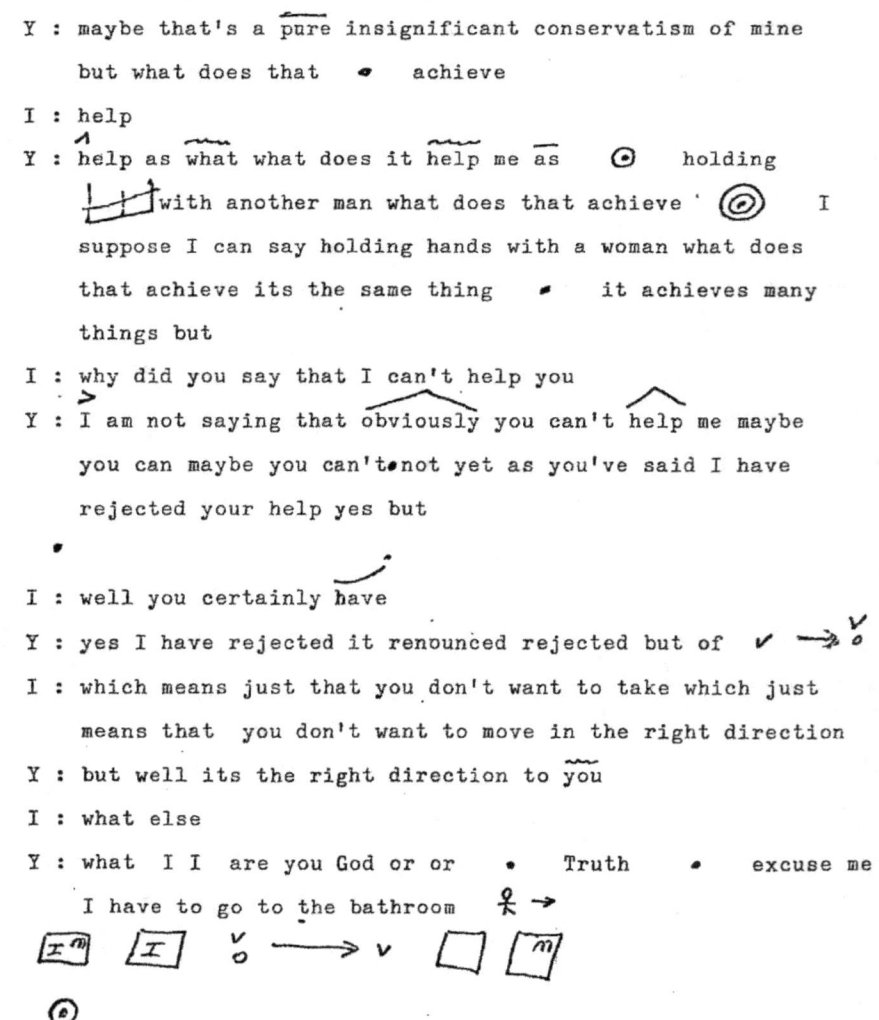

I : to help you

Y : what does that help me as

    •

I : warmth contact

Y : contact as what

I : what do you want•do you reject

Y : maybe that's a pure insignificant conservatism of mine
    but what does that • achieve

I : help

Y : help as what what does it help me as   ⊙   holding
    with another man what does that achieve ⊙ I
    suppose I can say holding hands with a woman what does
    that achieve its the same thing • it achieves many
    things but

I : why did you say that I can't help you

Y : I am not saying that obviously you can't help me maybe
    you can maybe you can't•not yet as you've said I have
    rejected your help yes but

    •

I : well you certainly have

Y : yes I have rejected it renounced rejected but of ✓ —➔ ○

I : which means just that you don't want to take which just
    means that you don't want to move in the right direction

Y : but well its the right direction to you

I : what else

Y : what I I are you God or or • Truth • excuse me
    I have to go to the bathroom ➔

I : what if I said yes

Y : ♀→   if you said yes you were God or Truth what

I : what if I said yes

Y : ℓ   (↶)(I'd probably laugh)

I : maybe you have to

Y : ⊬

I : sorry

Y : could be   ⊬   yes maybe   ⊬

I : maybe

Y : yes maybe

I : no no that I know   ⊬

Y : yes maybe the truth and   ⊬   ŏ→v   my ignorance

maybe   ⊬   ⊬   barely coming through to myself

I : well   _sss T rew_

◘

   sss T pla   I-boy Hi-boy Kim   here I will try and get

hold of you later in the week again otherwise give me a

call the best time for me is hmm late at night bye

I : ♀→

   ⊞ ⊚ ℓ ☐   ŏ→ v   _sss (T)_

tell me one thing do you think that you will have another

opportunity like this again in your life

Y : many

I : you will

Y : opportunity of what

I : finding out helping

Y : myself

I : of a rel of a relationship like me   ●   of a person like me

Y : why not ⊙   ▲   you speak in pure

I : impure

Y : in pure

I : Hullo ● message service ● oh O.K. just mention to Kim when he calls in that I called him back I got I just missed his message he can call me back anytime its his lover I hullo I can hardly hear you yes I I ♪ uminm that was to Copenhagen

Y : a heaven of a place to be your lover is in Copenhagen

I : sorry ● a heaven of a place to be ● he phoned I should have ● what do you uhm do you reject being homosexual

Y : yes because I can't see it as natural ● its not natural ● personally I like women ' ↗ s myself

I : you have never slept with a guy

Y : yes

I : you have slept with a guy

Y : yes

I : you have slept with a guy

Y : yes

I : and

Y : I have experienced both

I : and

Y : I prefer woman V ⇒ o I don't know

I : what did you do do with the guy

Y : what did I do as in what

I : as in physical interrelation

Y : contact

I : what sort of contact

Y : I leave it to your imagination ● actually

I : well you can but if you want me to help you in a
    particular form it might

Y : I am getting a bit crushed on what is this help here
              what is it achieving   are you
    saying that I am subliminally subliminally a homosexual
    subliminally a homosexual

I : do you think I am saying that

Y : possibly actually

I : which you reject

Y : the point No I don't reject it because I think there
    are subliminal feelings in all of us and I think I think
           personally there are subliminal feelings
    in myself that I am homosexual but I am not   oh
    fuck it   V → o I am not

I : you think that guys want some physical homosexual
    contact with you   holding hands   with

Y : that is my ignorance because

I : oh but you were obviously thinking of something

Y : because yes I would have to think I would have to think
           subliminal subliminal homosexual contact

I : and

Y : and that maybe my ignorance because maybe I ascribe that
    to you   oh fuck it   I'm sorry   and
    maybe I should not ascribe that to you but I did

I : its OK if you want to   sure   did you think
    that is all that is wanted

Y : whether that be all that is wanted or whether that be
    part of you that wanted it or whether that be an

insignificant amount of you that wanted it is

insignificant to me   •   its not what I want

I : really what do you want

Y :   as in what

I : sorry

Y : as in what • a person • or as in

I : no from me

Y : or as in a loved individual or from you

I : uhm

Y : Oh from you well I mean   •   I just met you randomly

  •   at a   •   a play © I think • no

I : no what

Y : describe for your help I can say

I : but how can I help you

Y :   yes how can you help me that is the question

   I am asking now

I : I can't help you

Y : yes you can't help me

I : I can help you

Y : you can but you can't

I : no I can help you

Y : you can you   can but you can't

I : why can't I

Y : because it is an extremely large block   between

   us

I : between us • in what way

Y : my preference

I : to what

Y : to a conservative type of life

I : which is what well you know its not and I know
    its not and I know its not

Y : yes words

I : you want to play words I can play words

Y : sorry I forgot you somewhat of a writer yourself
         words mean nothing

I : I and I can run rings around you when it comes to
    words but   but it is not me

Y : I've already its its already been proved been proven
    been proved whatever you are your grammatic senses

I : I can run rings around you when it comes to integrity

Y : Integrity honesty words yes maybe you are the perfect
    being compared to me

I : no

Y : maybe maybe   maybe

I : but

Y : but it means its irrelevant to me its nothing to me

I : but

Y : no

I : no what

Y : I don't see your world as true   no

I : you don't see my world as true   what is my world

Y : something I don't understand

I : so how can you see it if you don't understand it

Y :   enlighten me   a homosexual hetersexual
    I mean what   what life is that

I : who is a homosexual are you saying I am a homosexual

Y : No

I : what are you saying

Y : with tendencies what is wha is why are you why OK
I have to say you are a heterosexual actually ● but
why would you ask me to hold your hand what do you gain
from that what do I gain from that ● what what do I
gain from holding you in this in this in this confined
space as being a father son image as being a a oh I
forget the term but maybe its irrelevant
this is a telephone answering machine

I : just one second please· □ Kim ja ja
no bother ya ya I'll tell you later OK bye bye
what are you thinking

Y : hm

I : what are you thinking

Y : about what

I : what could it have gained I tell you what I thought
it could have gained by the way

Y : what

I : (s)(some sort of warmth)·(some sort of opening up) of
you some sort

Y : yes that is precisely what it could not have gained
you knew you knew that yourself that it could
not have gained that

I : how come

Y : much because you knew that I was conservatively
involved in that

I : how do you mean conservatively

Y : you knew as well as anybody that if you would sit down
with me and hold my hand you knew that I would consider
that homosexual ● you knew that you knew that as soon
as you closed those curtains that I would consider

that homosexual

I : I didn't think

Y : because I because I I have had an experience with
homosexuals ● so to speak

I : tell me about it

Y : because in my uhm in Solid

I : in what

Y : in Solid Daland the city there is a city in Daland
Daland Daland I went to see Castle Maidenhead one day
and I was hitchhiking to see it and I was hitching out
to see it and and I happened to get a ride with the curator
of well Castle Maidenhead and he happened to give me a
his own um he happened to give me a free ticket to go
and see Castle Maidenhead and everything like that and
then later on in the day when I was found round the
costume gallery I met up with him again and he asked me
out for a drink and then I questioned his integrity
and he offered me a place to stay his place and so he
was very kind about it all and he offered to take me to
the QE 100 the next day to give me the best ride I could
either to the North or the South either or which way
I wanted to go and so I and so I said sure and took
myself out of the hostel went you know to his place and
it was a nice bed we went out that night we went drinking
we ate at his house and then ah eventually ended up at
his place again drinking you know in the middle of the
night you know he he ends up he ends up in my bed too
ohh I just don't get on with that at all and you know
what he thinks to be sexual emancipation or sexual

conservatism or whatever well I told him I told him
I am not a homosexual and I said I could and I said
would he please leave

I : and he did

Y : yes he did

I : interesting is that your homosexual experience

Y : well my homosexual experience my second homosexual
experience while travelling

I : don't don't why make me angry don't don't don't throw
these sarcastic looks at me

Y : sarcastic looks

I : Yeh

Y : sarcastic looks

I : Yeh

Y : I threw a sarcastic look at you

I : because I 🔲 shadow

Y : 　　　　　🔲　　　　 I shadow 🔲 I maybe you don't deserve
that I am sorry I'm very sorry for putting sarcastic
looks at you but my experience at home and abroad 🔲
that anyone who has ever been extreemly kind to me has
been a homosexual

I : OK fair enough so you think I am OK OK

Y : No I am sorry maybe a sarcas I mean you don't deserve
that maybe maybe lets say but I am sorry

I : maybe I do

Y : maybe you do maybe you don't I'm sorry but

I : try try and cut it out try and relax try and cut out
that hardness or that sarcasm cause whatever you say

I'll take it whether it is sarcastically said or
what or not you don't have to

Y : (s)(well I don't have the education to be pure)

I : maybe you do maybe you are very angry about what has
happened but don't project that on me you can if you
want to but it irritates me slightly

Y : I'm sorry

I : OK and your second homosexual

Y : you have the right you have the right to be you know
to be

I : well maybe I do or maybe I don't but it just so
happens that as you may or may not like certain people
doing certain things to you I don't like people
projecting that's all attributing that sort of thing

Y : OK OK I would agree with you fully in fact I would not
like that other individual projecting it on me

I : so your second when was this Castle Maidenhead thing
how long ago was that

Y : only a a few few weeks ago but

I : that was the first homosexual experience

Y : in Backarub

I : sorry

Y : in Ygoslavia my second which was not so much pronounced

I : that was more recent

Y : no

I : that was before

Y : it was much longer ago I was in the very last few days
of February it was more of a travelling experience
actually because I couldn't find a place to stay in

Backarub and I had to spend this uhm in a private
family ┗┤ what they call subra subra there and
this guy happened to be a he was about twenty years old
and he happened to be a magician in the nearby cafe we
drank an awful lot and he drank too much wine he tried
quite a bit 🔲 with me 🔲 and 🔲 as in hands .
movement you understand me

I : tried quite a bit with you

Y : as

I : gently gently I know this is personal to you and I

Y : he tried well the expression in the States is quote
get down my pants unquote but a girl usually says that
to a guy and   ·

I : he tried to get down your pants

Y : yeah

I : how far did he get

Y : not very far because I just pushed him off

I : how far

Y : you want need his excuse well first he used um he got
uh tiny porno magazine and pointed he wanted to know
the english names for parts of the male and female
anatomy that was when I learnt my first Yugoslav words
for well actually I knew how to say yes and thank you
and he wanted to know the girl's female orifex was and
and what the male's protrusion was and everything like
that and I just told him the scientific names

I : you are being very clinical now you realise that

Y : yes I am being very clinical of course sorry that I am
very very conservative too in this sense his big term

was pitchka which means in Yugoslav slang for what the
Americans would call cunt which is   •   you know that
in the english sense but   •   we used to laugh he tried
well he did a trick on me me he said he went to show
how me how to how to he lights light bulb with
electricity of an individual he put his hand on the
individual spot and he proceeded to scoop down into my
pants and I pushed him off and he tried it again and I
just pushed him off and said that and that it was late
that night thank god he didn't share the guy at Castle
Maidenhead actually shared my bed I woke up with his
fucking arm around me

•

I : you didn't like that

Y : No I didn't like it at all

I : why

Y : because I don't feel anything for it

I : or because you didn't want to feel anything for it

Y : maybe I didn't maybe I didn't feel for it but I didn't
feel anything for it so to speak period and and I told
to leave me alone I said I am not a homosexual my exact
words exact words for him I am not a homosexual

I : but you surely are not a homosexual

Y : yes I am sure

I : so what's your problem

Y : I told him to leave me alone and he just

I : no no what's your problem why are you so what

Y : because I fear I could <u>become</u> one that I could become one

I : If

Y : yes a lot of things

I : if what

Y : if I could never relate myself totally to a girl world

I : would it hurt you if you were a homosexual

Y : yes

I : why

Y : very much so   and again you are asking absurd questions because

I : whats an absurd question

Y : because it does hurt me it would hurt me

I : why

Y : because its just not natural

I : why is it not natural

Y : because in my opinion (S) (conservative old fashioned) whatever the term you wish to use its not its not right

I : what is not right

Y : for a male and a male to be sexually involved with each other

I : why

Y : because its not

I : thats not a good enough reason

Y : pardon

I : thats not a good enough reason

Y : maybe not a good enough reason but I agree with the Japenese in representing nature and nature is for the proliferation of nature proliferation of life

I : no

Y : no (;) no maybe maybe and maybe not maybe so and maybe this that the other maybe a whole lot of whole whole

fucking lot of things but there is one thing I do •
quote believe unquote in and that's male and female
maybe I take it too romantically maybe I take it too
absurdly maybe I take it too too

I : you know male female means very many things it means
male female if you want to sexually which is a very trite
way of looking at the world

Y : extreemly trite but

I : no but let me finish Male female can also mean certain
types of personalities as the Chinese think as
everyone thinks they do not designate sex it is
characteristically soft warm receiving giving

Y : bitter hard distressful

I : sorry bitter hard ro not bitter not hard I mean ones
giving ones receiving that is the whole principle of the
Ying and the Yang it is not male female in the sense
you think or what most people think male sexual organ
and female sexual organ it can be but that is just the
minor part

Y : yes that is just what I am saying that's what I'm
saying I don't understand everything I don't understand
everything but I'm but I'm no I'm not homosexual I
know I am not I'm

I : but you are wrong of course

Y : how I'm wrong of course as you say as you project as
you wish to say I mean thats

I : neither here nor there ✦

Y : I mean thats thats your suggestion but

I : if you are not a homosexual by the way why did you try it

Y : I did when I was once quite where was I fifteen
    fourteen fifteen

I : fifteen you did so

Y : I had sex with a man and I just did not like it

I : well how who was the man

Y : it was an age old orphan in my hometown

I : how old was the man older

Y : younger yeah a year younger than I was two years younger
    something like that

I : and what did you do   •   one of the reasons why I
    closed the curtains by the way just to make it darker
    so that there would be more light let in so that you
    wouldn't necessarily feel that I would be embarrassing
    you and you could be embarrassed aside from the fact

Y : help me to what are you're saying that what I am is a
    homosexual that wishes to uncover the curtain and wishes
    to come out of the corner

I : maybe if you want to see it that way but sometimes its
    dark to give at to see and its necessary to see

Y : maybe I do not wish to necessarily to see maybe I

I : maybe

Y : maybe I wish wish to cloud myself to the fact that
    subliminally I am a homosexual subliminally but to the
    fact that I do not wish to be one

I : well then that's another question entirely

Y : another question entirely

I : then you need psychiatric help

Y : well of course maybe I need psychiatric help

I : or maybe love

Y : love from whom

I : from anyone anyone who can understand you

Y : maybe there is not anyone who understands me

I : No I understand you

Y : Oh you understand me to your projection of understanding

I : call it what you like

Y : I'm sorry   sarcasm now   •   No   •   I can't accept
the homosexual existence

I : no I don't think you can you either commit suicide or
you can become a psychopath

Y : that's quite true

I : sure

Y : nawh

I : or you can ask for help if you really want

Y : but your help your help   is   •   is to
accept homosexuality

I : no not to help you to accept homosexuality

Y : then I don't understand what your help is

I : my help is to help you whatever you are

Y : by similar sex to hold hands in

I : that's just the start of dialogue

Y : in Trafalgar Square say we'll just go out and sing gay
little songs or something

I : no no my help is for you just to be a little bit more
gentle than you are being as a start and to just open
up a bit more than you are being now and to accept
yourself eventually

Y : accept myself as what

I : what you are

Y : what am I

I : well that's for you to find out

Y : yes but you are suggesting that I am subliminally a homosexual

I : I am not suggesting anything by the way do you want more wine I can open another bottle

Y : I don't know its up to you

I : red or white

Y : I'm quite a drunk actually

I : yes that's one of the symptoms as well

Y : what's that supposed to mean   ●   that an alcoholic needs alcohol

I : No an alcoholic yes an alcoholic needs alcohol in order to avoid

Y : true

I : to shut off to cloud his mind so where he can't feel things

Y : so I

I : you don't want to feel things do you

Y : I don't yes   ●   So you say I'm an alcoholic that cannot feel things or does not want to or does not wish to feel things

I : correct

Y : open another bottle because I am

I : yes

Y : I because I am an alcoholic and I don't wish to feel things

I : maybe I don't wish to open another bottle

Y : that's that's up to you

I : Isn't it sad that you're an alcoholic with potential

```
Y : am I sad
        ʌ
I : It sad
      ≝
Y : It it     •   Isn't it sad
      ≝   ≝
I : yeh cut out this hard edge really cut it out I know it's
Y : this negation this
I : it's ultimately using your ultimate defences
Y : what am I defending against
I : yourself
Y : what are you suggesting I am then I am defending
    against
I : you are being very loud and aggressive
  •
Y : yes I am
I : and I don't like that in anybody especially people who
    get drunk and become loud and aggressive
Y : you wish me to leave
I : another defence no I don't wish you to leave if I
    wished you to leave I'd ask you to leave
Y : well then what if I'm becoming  becoming a loud and
    aggressive why don't you wish me to leave because its
    a very     •     distasteful
I : because I understand why you are becoming loud and
    aggressive what I am trying to say to you is that it is
    unnecessary whatever you say I understand it I get
    the message
Y : how can you understand
I : because I have got that much more experience because I'm
Y : you're what about 25  7 years on me
```

I : yes ● but I have also experienced a lot understand
a lot

Y : then what becomes right and wrong in seven years in
seven years

I : because I took the roads that you are not prepared to
take and I don't know if you will ever take them

Y : probably not

I : well that's uh uh

Y : probably

I : well then no one can help you

Y : yes because I am a failure in that respect because

I : you will not be honest

Y : yes because I won't be honest you've taken the roads
as to what to /what ● have you taken

I : I took those roads such as they are such as I took them
of trying to be honest to myself

Y : honest to what

I : to myself

Y : to yourself but as in relation to what

I : to anything

Y : to anything what is anything

I : to human all to human

Y : being is a

I : oh come on

Y : is a horrible word

I : what thing is a horrible word

Y : I

I : no no no gently gently easy to ● anything in my
relationship to myself first

Y : first

I : I first I first of course if I can't be honest to myself
    who can I be honest to

Y : Okay well take that as given quote given unquote we'll
    take that now   𝑜   now

I : gently gently

Y : what's the next relation

I : anything   𝑜   people   𝑜   other people

Y : what other people

I : males females   𝑜   art   𝑜   anything anything just
    as they came to me

Y : then what then what what did you do what did you
    achieve as truth

I : I'm not sure what truth is

Y : well I'm sorry its a poor question but did you achieve
    what as truth to you

I : that I am honest

Y : honest to whom

I : to anything everything to anything anything what

Y : what do you what do you think of yourself as

I : decent reliable

Y : reliable

I : sincere

Y : sincere

I : and very very intelligent

Y : intelligent

I : well that's another aspect of honesty

Y : well I agree with your intelligence but maybe I am

I : and very perceptive

Y : perceptive ⊘ perceptive

I : I can see through shit very easily

Y : through shit ⊘ but you consider what is shit

I : dishonesty

Y : dishonesty and

I : masks

Y : masks masks well what mask have you put on to prove
    you're true

I : I have not put up any that's why I'm true ⊘ what
    you see is what I am ⊘ of course that depends on
    what you can give at to see donner à voir à toi même

Y : which is which is a total reflection upon my own me

I : no

Y : oh my dishonesty

I : exactly ⊘ if you see that I have some homosexual
    closing the curtains to rip you off and get you into bed
    that's maybe what you think

Y : that is total dishonest though

I : not on my part

Y : it's on my part

I : you asked me why I closed the curtains and I told you
    very honestly if you didn't ask me I didn't have to
    tell you about it

Y : well why did you close the curtains

I : well I told you if you don't believe me that's OK

Y : to create an what an atmosphere for me to what
    ⊘

I : I told you you were not listening not to create an

atmosphere for but for two reasons firstly you asked
me to help you I said I did not know how but that I
thought that this is one of the ways certainly I learnt
something   * I learnt something about you that was
very helpful and it did help me

Y : maybe its very ugly but

I : it's not very ugly the second thing was to make to
make things   * certainly you may have thought whatever
you think I am sure you did

Y : I can assure you   ~~++++~~   actually

I : listen

Y : thought that when you closed the curtains

I : I didn't think that actually I didn't think that you
would be that base I didn't think that you would be that low

Y : you didn't think I would be that low I mean come on who
else would you think that   * I mean do you think
that I mean you're talking you're talking irrelevantly
to some one at a theatre our of pure irrelevancy and
that you are talking to them out of pure irrelevancy then
you're speaking to them at pure irrelevancy to talk to
them about themselves which is pure irrelevancy to your
closing the curtains which is pure irrelevancy another
pure irrelevancy   * what do you think what is that
other individual that you're talking to going to think

I : what does he

Y : he's going to think the fucking worst

I : what

Y : the fucking worst to me is homosexuality

I : well then you don't have to come

Y : I didn't have to ~~but~~ but I was curious

I : as to what

Y : as to curious

I : have you ever kissed a guy

Y : nNnno

I : tell me what happened with this guy at school that
you said you had

Y : I never kissed him

I : what did you do

Y : it was pure organic

I : what do you mean by pure organic

Y : the word organic I mean

I : you had sex together

Y : yeah we had sex together

I : how what sex

Y : animalistic

I : well what were you naked together

Y : naked yes naked together

I : he touched you

Y : he touched me and I touched him

I : did you come

Y : yes we both did

I : how

Y : as in how what I mean how

I : well how did he did you jerk him off did he jerk you off
as the Americans say

Y : it was neither or nor

I : well how were you lying

Y : no

I : how

Y : I was no he was on top of me it was both ways actually
    him on top of me and me on top of him it was never
    either or   •   but hell this is

I : how many years ago

Y : I was twelve years old   •   yea so what   •   probably
    he was ten   •   never nor

I : and since then you have never come with a guy

Y : yeah   •   what makes that so pretty important
    •   or of subliminal importance   ⊙   is
    that a necessitation of truth

I : why did you want to leave by the way

Y : because I just don't understand what you want

I : you don't understand what I want

Y : no there are two sides to everything no I still don't
    know the reason why you questioning me questioned me
    maybe from a professional viewpoint maybe end up as a
    few lines in a play or maybe I'll end up as nothing but
    but

I : maybe you'll end up as a lover

Y : no no I doubt that no still don't understand what
    is your motivation

I : becuase you don't understand that is why you wanted to
    leave

Y : yes which is a total enactment of my personality if I
    don't understand something I will to evade it as you

say evasion quote evasion unquote and I will and I'll
do that to the end of time

I : well then I can't help you no-one can help you

Y : that's right you just threw up your hands right there
symbolic as hell as it could be   because I will
evade it   .   because I will evade myself
because I will evade everything because I'm being loud
and forceful and stupid and anything else that you
want to say

I : don't you want to be helped

Y : listen why should I worry with it now

I : well why now there and just now yes

Y : hm

I : why now no and just now yes

Y : just now as in long ago now or

I : ah don't play games

Y : play games

I : why now no why don't you want to be helped now

Y : and a few minutes ago yes

I : right

Y : maybe I don't understand you or myself or myself in
relation to you or maybe a lot of things   ○   maybe
a lot of things   ○   as what you are calling for
your great truth truth ⊡ honesty

I : you're not very honest but anyway
   ○

Y : yes I am not very honest but I don't know if you are
either

I :

Y : pardon

I : I am I am and I know you know you're not and you're not
that's the only difference

Y : well hell supreme   I don't know if I am anymore

I : what dishonest

Y : dishonest honest where's that terminology quote
exclamation point naw   it doesn't mean anything
anymore   no way yah true truth bullshit
truth and untruth (r)(it does not mean anything)'extension
progression projection hey you're talking rubbish I mean
you can take it as rubbish

I : how come you have changed from five minutes ago from
being rather gentle rather sincere I think   thought
to becoming so very aggressive loud not the wine because
you have not had any more wine

Y : it is not the wine

I : just the fact that I attempted to   has caused this

Y : it caused this   yet you placed me in a totally
defenceless point view point

I : defenceless viewpoint

Y : no you placed me on a view point where you are on on
the offensive and now I am on the defensive

I : you on the defensive yes but when you're on the defensive
you become loud and aggressive

Y : yes

I : I know that's why I did not throw you out that's what
I said I knew you're on the defensive

Y : I still don't understand your attempt at   ~~HH~~   it
just doesn't stupidly maybe   •   maybe it does

I : you don't understand it because love or affection or
anything like you don't understand

Y : no I don't understand love or affection I've admitted
⌐that I've admitted that a thousand times I don't know
anything about it I don't understand what that achieves
in love in affection

I : well I know

Y : what ⌐i^m⌐   •   yeah well yeah   .

I : well if you don't want to be helped then that's it
•

Y : exactly

I : sorry

Y : suitable thing

I : what

Y : I've said whatever you say

⌐m⌐

I : its not whatever I want to say you've got a mind you can
think for yourself

Y : yeah I can picture it for myself   .

I : such as   •   success or suicide

Y : some say its the best

I : it is never the best

Y : why

I : what a waste

Y : what am I wasting

I : you're wasting a lot

Y :   wasting nothing I'm wasting nothing

I : you're wasting a lot of potential

Y : potentialities is all we are

I : then you're wasting what you are

Y : then I'm nothing in the first place

I : putting it this way yea I mean a why is that you have

    such an anti-reaction against homosexuality from your

    parents

Y : maybe my mother maybe to me its its unnatural

I : is love unnatural

Y : love . you talk of love ◁   oh oh god love unnatural

I : is it

Y : is love unnatural you are asking

I : is love unnatural yes or no

Y : from what standpoint

I : any standpoint is love unnatural yes or no

Y : no

I : it isn't unnatural

Y : but sexual love

I : come on sexual what do you mean by sexual

Y : aaw come on what are you asking love is a friendship or

    love as some v ⟶ ö

I : so you could love a guy

Y : as a friend as anyone • ja ja   ja ja

I : the time is an old illusion ◦ you might have

Y : of course not   ✎   why not

I : of course I am not going to let you touch me

Y : and that that wouldn't let any other man touch me

I : I'm not any other man oh well

Y : I suppose that you figure that if you touch me that I
    am in love with you   ✎   then why do you wish to
    touch me

I : would it help you

Y : help me to what

I : to other things

Y : to know what

I : I don't know

Y : if you don't know ✝✝

I : sorry   ⊙   its not irrelevant   ●   I know   ✎   you
    know

Y : who knows hell I'll probably enjoy it but it's not going
    to mean anything

I : to whom

Y : to whom to you to me to its not going to mean anything
    to you

I : you don't think so

Y : very much so

I : you could be wrong

Y : I am not wrong

I : not wrong

Y :   ✎   that's one thing I know I am not wrong about
    the uncertaintly of it all   ●   but I leave here tonight
    its not going to mean a thing

I : to me

Y : to you its not going to mean a thing you're going
    to talk to your friends you're going to talk to
    whoever is going to produce your 丰 next such and such
    a matter of time you're going to V ⟶ ᵛₒ

I : you think so

Y : of course so

I : its got nothing to mean with words that are meaningful
    to me to plays would it mean anything to you

Y : why would it mean anything to me

I : will it mean anything to you

Y : will it mean anything to me for the next week maybe
    because I stay here and then I leave then I do go back
    home to all that bullshit that I came that I left from

I : its your choice

Y : of course its my choice ● maybe at 18 its the
    only choice I've got right now

I : well are there any other choices

Y : ah

I : I really really wish ● with a lot for a with a fair
    degree of sincerity

Y : sincerity of what
    ●

I : these things don't mean a thing a fair degree of sincerity
    from your point of view from my point of view from a
    general human point of view from truth from everything
    if you'd let me ● you
    ◉

Y : help me to what
    ●

I : to

Y : hm

I : we can go round and round in circles

Y : I know we can [●] I have observed that for quite a
while now means nothing

I : importance

Y : it means nothing to what you attribute truth now

I : which is

Y : what you attribute to truth is nothing but what
anybody else attributes to truth

I : continue

Y : no no

I : no no you will not have many opportunities like this
I don't think there you are

Y : many opportunities ⋊   ●   you draw   ⋊

I : what is wrong with your being a homosexual

Y : [●]   what is wrong

I : it may just be a phase

Y : a phase ●   what is right with it

I : it depends what you need or how about because God wills
it

Y : oh oh god will it what god wills it that's bullshit what
bullshit god wills anything the sky is blue the earth
is green

I : because of what you are

Y : maybe its nothing

I : you are sure

Y : yeah

I : you know you are wrong

Y : so your entire purpose in life giving to sit on this
planet to find one 18 year old who has ⊎ decided
that he is not homosexual but its your purpose to find

out that he is actually

I : not its not my purpose at all

Y : no

I : there's a purpose as a purpose if you want help there
   to find out the truth

Y : the truth to find out that I am truthfully a homosexual

I : are you

Y : no

I : then you are not •   I reckon you now want to leave

Y : just looking at the time

I : you came so close to to someone

Y : yes but I am as I said I am a failure

I : only because you want to be

Y : that I want to be

I : want to be a failure

Y : yeah that's what I want

I : you don't want to be

Y : I said that I want to be

I : well its something going for you if you want to be
   as well

Y : pardon

I : you have a lot going for you if you want • to be
   as well

Y : want to be as in what •   a non failure

I : if you wanted to be yeah if you wanted to be you've
   got a lot going for you

Y : and I suppose what constitutes • (r)(wanted to be) is
   an admission of homosexuality I mean thats •   it seems

to be a key

I : cut out this word homosexuality its just a word

Y : yeh its just a word as everything else we've been
saying for the last couple of hours whatever its been

I : its what you are

Y : what I am what

I : thats all thats important what you are to admit to
the fact that you have feelings for men as well as for
women have you ever slept with a guy woman

Y : yes

I : when

I : Oh god I used to have a girlfriend I slept with all the
time   she's a year older than I am Swiss she goes
to school in where Virginia in a fact

I : this guy that you screwed sorry that you slept with
when you were ten he didn't screw you

Y : no

I : you didn't screw him

Y : no oh   god

I : oh god what

Y : god

I : why

Y : why I just told you

I : but what is the god exclamation for

Y : its an explanation without a point when something
absurd absurd

I : keep looking at the time

Y : uhm

I : why

Y : that figures ✏ a certain time that I should leave
so that I can make it back to the hostel

I ; what time should that be

Y : about 9.30 ten I guess I don't need a tube I guess
I can walk back

I : money

Y : no

I : why not

Y : nobody gives me anything

I : stu

Y : nobody gives me anything

I : why not why not

Y : because I make either my own way or I don't yeah I'll
be as stupid as I choose that's another choice we have

I : Al

Y : probably not no I should go out and commit suicide
probably should I must use that in a certain future
time

I : I hope you'll not

Y : I'll choose it its not that I choose what is best for me
✏

I : why not why no help

Y : what can you help me as

I : what ever you want to be

Y : I choose to be something different I choose

I : I don't choose you to be anything

Y : just let me choose what I want to be

I : what I choose you to be

Y : what do you envision as being

I : sorry

Y : what do you envision as being

I :

Y : no you don't no no

I : why no help

Y : why do I want you to help me

I : you want me to help you for many many reasons

Y : one of which is not the reason which I wish you'to

I : one of which is what

Y : one of which is not the reason you wish to help me

I : which is what

Y : guidance towards a certain thing which is

I : if you know that how else do you want help

Y : no

I : no what

Y : no is the answer to many things

I : that is not an answer to anything

Y : of course not

I : don't play these stupid games

Y : stupid yes

I : and

Y : no

I : so how else do you want me to help you

Y : no

I : what do you mean no you can't see any other way I can
   help you

Y : no

I : well then

Y : then

I : then what

Y : you can show me direction 🔲 you can do this you can
   do that

I : but

Y : direction

I : sorry

Y : I said not direction

I : how do you mean not direction

Y : because its something that I intimately fail at 🔲 yes
   there's no direction

I : I show you direction I don't show you direction so
   therefore I fail you

Y : I fail that myself but thats irrelevant yeah no now no
   no no no you cannot show me direction

I : why not

Y : because there is no direction to be shown 🔲 there is
   (s)(no direction to be shown)

I : of course there is

Y : which direction east west north or south

I : to yourself

Y : maybe I show myself many directions but

I : theres a revolution

Y : which

I : do you know there is a blank wall

Y : a blank wall

I : there are lots of directions

Y : empty space   many directions in which way

I : the right way its the only way

Y : the right ∘ what ✐ there's no way there's no
    way right is left left is right

I : yes there is but of course there is at a certain point

Y : why

I : because you know it

Y : because I know it

I : you know the way you are going at the moment is not the
    right direction so therefore that its

Y : so therefore what I've created a totally wrong direction

I : yes you have

Y : as in what

I : because you are just so crazy mixed up and confused
    and evasive and dishonest

Y : oh evasive dishonesty perfection morality oh god comments
    in your next play maybe

I : its not a play

Y : oh come on

I : what

Y : I said all humankind is a play ✐ its a stage a
    dream ⧠ No the hell it is mixed up ⧠ live in an
    illusion ⧠ dishonest ⧠ No I don't know exactly
    what truth you projected on me everywhere

I : the truth

Y : the truth you are the commanding god

I : don't be so trite

Y : trite trite quote trite unquote what is trite it is
    a terminology a truth that you make up

I : you are really that desperate

Y : yes maybe I am that desperate but you can't show me
    the truth

I : I can I

Y : naw naw can you show me one truth or your truth maybe
    its true or I'm just totally stupid or not true

I : you want it or you don't want it

Y : me   me may be   be

I : well its a start put it that way its a start

Y : a start to what

I : to the road

Y : to re-evangelise the truth

I : oh come on I'm not what is it a reborn christian
    anyway

Y : no

I : why not

Y : no

I : are you hungry by the way

Y : pardon

I : are you hungry

Y : yes very

I : what would you like to eat

Y : what do you mean what

I :   some sandwhiches some ham some bread honey fruit

Y : ah as to what I must walk

I : why

Y : because when I walk I feel more disillusioned and
when I feel more disillusioned then I

I : then you what

Y : I said I walk further first I feel more disillusioned
then when I walk walk come back

I : you'll feel better to

Y : yes

I : go for a eighteen minute odd walk and then you can come
back and have something meaty

Y : OK be about a half an hour walk

I : hm

Y : I'll come back

Y :

mother will they put me in the firing line
mother am I really dying
hush now baby don't you cry .
mamas gonna make all of your
Nightmares come true
Mamas gonna put all of her fears into you
Mamas gonna keep you right here
Under her wing
She won't let you fly but she might let you sing
Mama will keep baby cosy and warm
Ooooh Babe Ooooh Babe Ooooh Babe
Of course mam'll help build the wall
Hush now baby , baby don't you cry
Mamas gonna check out all your girl friends for
you

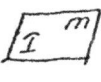

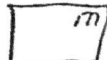

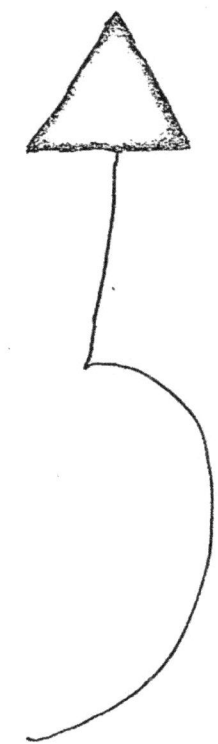

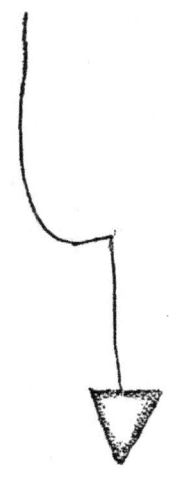

Y : terrible ● hand in hand ● on the ground
● hands to hands ● fire ● voices ● of
course ● its fine ● problem ● of course it
is ● I know ● hetr a little girlfriend said ah
help ● help ● helped ● marriage ● on
the ground hands to hands fire of course helped marriage ● noises
yes yes yes yes ● arms around me ● very
warm drive failure ● fall between them show me
how to I'm quite sure I can how to pardon say don't
● what its mean to me pardon yes but its
exploration of sexual feeling

I : why

Y : because I am not in that period

I : what period are you in

Y : no feeling and

I : some feeling

Y : No it is not for a girl or not and so how do you feel
not pure common and so how do you explain naturalism
● what is nature natural

I : read a thesis on homosexuality

Y : yeah

I : one condition

Y : what   •   I told you that   because I am not a homosexual   •   its a waste of time do you waste your entire time or is it just just in

I : in end I wasted my entire time because

Y : because how help you should have walked out   •   sure   I didn't hear a damn thing

I : it was a miscalculation

Y : I didn't necessarily feel it do you think or things are different now oh god feel me no feed me I said oh feed me as you do with it   •   its not here or there   •   bang of course I am I am   •   then then judging what misjudging me disillusionment on my part projection of yourself on me to me disillusionment my part projection on me what achieved   •   and so what what have you achieved   •   in the end terrible of course I agree nothing of any value value to me your idea of help is so so what help to me idea of dissilusionment my part projection on me what achieved help idea means nothing nothing your idea of help means me as condemning me but at the same point you are   •   condemning yourself your idea of help is as   as so what help me to become as what as an individual as me Why as this as Why ah ah what is the idea of help can't look into me and see it means nothing what I look at sorry your idea of help is not to   •   help me as what as individual

as why you can't look into me and see what I look at
as help your idea of help achieve as I don't follow
me I don't follow me me you this that yes yes maybe
you should look at me I suppose the nearest truth is a
best thing see page 27 B pardon pardon

I : we uh were talking about some

Y : I'm very bad to be so late

I : Uhm we were talking about

Y : I just don't like my voice

I : do you remember what you were talking about

Y : why I was afraid about others the others yes because my
relationship with others have always been always been
very tenuous very tenuous   *   very unstable always
an unstable always an instability

$\left[\begin{array}{c}\mathcal{I}\end{array}\right]^{m}$

very uh very with the way I have felt as an individual
to add you can pick my two best friends in the States
that that they are the only two that are relevant you
know   *   I'm the only two that I would give a damn
makes an expression like $\boxed{m}$

I : one of the guys

Y : was kind always you know your best friend always boosts
you always said to me everything you do is right you know
ya yes you're right and only a few times we had problems
with each other then the other guy I know is very
satirical of me he's very sarcastic of me lets say and
he and I get along very well because you you know I
know he knows me very well $\boxed{\bullet}$ and its just because
its irrelevant to your

I : its nothing really relevant is it it just means that

that you ahm still skirting

Y : words

I : which also means that you have another escape

Y : hide

I : yes I know you are an escapist that

Y : why

I : avoidance

Y : what avoid it yeah you noticed that very easily
right on why do you think

I : its very easy for you to say why or p or q

Y : why why p equals q want any help maybe help idea
maybe   do that ok can pardon hmm   a you're
young pardon yeah a song what if brain not understand
of course now he's sexual of course yes   yes thats
possible yes the fact that I'm gay well I am I am gay not
gay appears your weather I am or not the whole idea
  he the constant worry that I might be oh no
the question is if you are then there's no problem yeah
I guess central what more than the perfect man   oh
fuck so getting back to the entire argument running
away never get off the ground   honesty is
  honesty is honesty is being pretty straight
about everything maybe I'll even get off the deal but
I'd rather not rather not sleep in that sort of world
I'd rather not rather be a failure than gay one denotes
one one denotes the other in an and stroke or situation
ya ya what ya   ya indeed indeed well thats sex
  meaning   oh jeez youre talking first

terms maybe ya what its just my nature conquest true
now now it is a lie honest something that is lost lost
keep it in front of you clubs and bars can I meet the
right person can I live it [symbol] can't each other three
dead the views Oh god so do you agree its dead once I
admit and attain that a homosexual human being that
maybe I sure pure [symbol] improve [symbol] and I'd have
success and of course its an absurd relationship
because its admitting I'm homosexual if I admit to myself
that I am homosexual which is ● I suppose a
calculator out later one letting on because a group
essential homosexual I'll become so non-conformist
I'm a homosexual I'm a

I : no no not necessarily right that p equals q but that what

Y : p always equals q ● why I feel why I don't know I
feel that I have always gotten better off being alone

I : and its important so so a lot of people feel never so
alone as when they are with people

Y : oh that a can

I : yea its neither here nor there for instance I think
you feel under pressure almost under an attack

Y : yeah I can see

I : by inter human relationships or by people

Y : △ thats quite right on I do feel under attack
I feel plagued

I : you feel

Y : plagued I'm being plagued by other people

I : why in what way

Y : because they interfere with my my direction I'd
say ● I don't know

I : they interfere with your direction no

Y : but I

I : no I don't thats true

Y : let me tell you because there's truth in it no I feel
I do feel that people interfere with my directions
because let me clarify that

I : what do you feel   is it a principle that people
should not interfere with your direction to help you in
any way

Y : it is possible that I can be aided to achieve what I am to
to achieve that is it

I : probably yes

Y : is it possible someone out there must be true

I : well truth is what you wish to know or not

Y : true

I : do you wish to be aided or not

Y : that is the bitter I mean that is the question because
I mean do I wish to be aided do do I I can't say I can't
say for sure do I wish to be do I wish to find out
everything on my own and say that there is influence in
other people because   no I   I used to always
want to be done by myself and from there on   my
future plans work   finding myself on my own is
always very important to me

I : hmm   what if you want   what if you come
to a point where you want progress

Y : staysis stasis

I : its irrelevant if you don't think you're at there
do you think you're at there

Y : staysis yeah

I : you are at a point of stasis

Y : I am at a point at point over a long time over the
summer I felt an extreemly strong staysis stasis of
achieving nothing and

I : so do you think   •   you want someone to help you

Y : it seems to me that   •   hell it's very important
yes I am at the point where I can't find who or what
the hell I am   •   someone   •   hell I have
to be maybe I intellectualise a lot of romantic idealism
•   in me

I : such as what

Y : oh its difficult to describe

I : such as what there's nothing stupid about being romantic

Y : I think it is

I : being romantic.

Y : romantic about   •   romance

I : what do you mean

Y : still it's above me untouchable but wantable point the
getting back to the existential belief in goal the goal
that I created I cannot reach   •   Virginia   •   I
look at woman that way very much

I : You you what do you mean by what you said or what I
think you said that having someone help you conflicts
with your ideals with your romantic ideals and with
your romantic ideals being your romantic ideal about
woman how do you mean by that why should someone

helping you conflict with that

Y : no notion

I : sorry I found a relation

Y : yes sure yes hm you writers hmm relation ● oh ● you
are trying to relate to me sometimes I started talking
on a different ● I like ⊙ I think I think
what I want to say is that I feel my romantic ideals
conflict with my progress

I : what can I ask again your romantic ideals were

Y : when I am with women and ● first I am a
romantic

I : your romantic ideal about them and they would conflict
with what ⊡ with your progress

Y : yeah with progress because I feel I feel I am not
giving I don't feel I am giving them ● the other
affair hmm ⊙ ah ⊙ getting back to honesty I don't
feel I don't feel that I relate honestly to people that
● you know I always always say in terminology
if you look at an individual as an individual ● well
that sort of picture-image such as Napoleon that was
an image you know

I ; sorry

Y : I was just using that as an example an image uh I
didn't look at you as an individual the girl Manda and
uh I was using a romantic picture of her that I
created it was non-honest relationship to her and I
feel an honest human relationship is I can't express

myself in projection I know you hardly I know I
don't project well

I : uh uh you're wrong there you project god I wouldn't
be wasting my time no unless you projected something
that showed of integrity and honesty and sensitivity
but you also project other things   but that's a
little of reading between the lines   hm there
are other superficial projections which cut no ice with me

Y : external as in

I : well yes I mean what you project in you that's neither
here nor there for me anyway fair enough I'm talking
about completely different things your projection on
an internal level with people and we go to it for the
third time   and that's the last time and

Y : again evasion

I : yes uhm I will now I only do it three times because if
you don't go a bit closer on the third time it means you
don't really want to and I'm not one for pushing things
uhm its still you came out with it subconsciously uhm
let me just try and think a bit more   how do
you want to pro lets rephrase it how do
you want to progress   which also means you are at
a particular point where you feel you've got to progress

Y : progress or staysis

I : yea OK or whatever it is it's not a point you want
to be at now because there's no progress so where
where do you think you want to progress to

Y : conflicts with three sses at the end with a social
level

I : I don't follow you mean resolve conflicts on a social
level

Y : yes because I don't ● I can't handle society so
how will I progress how will I progress ● on a level
with a group of others how will I progress ● when
I dont conform because I dont want to conform

I : yes but what dont you want to conform in you conform
quite a lot on a social level since I met you

Y : oh well yeah yeah youre right but

●

I : why

Y : why

I : why do you have to conform and what do you have to
conform to

Y : to exist you have to conform

I : uhm to exist you have to be yourself

Y : oh there oh there's the romantic view that I always
write about ● myself ● is honestly no one
exists as an individual they all should exist that's
the point that you get to

I : why can't you exist as an individual

Y : because plagued you are plagued with the opinion
of the other

I : why should you be plagued by the opinions of others

Y : because of the other because the opinion of others
make you

I : no that they don't

Y : you make you yes individually yes you make you there
excuse me out there you don't make anything

I : do you have to make something out there or do you
    have to make something to yourself ◪ and don't you
    think that if you were more honest with yourself you'd
    be able to relate better out there

Y : yes but what what will I create out there a facade

I : what you are creating out there a dishonest facade

Y : yes I am I am but it's something I'm attempting not
    to create but I

I : but

Y : I don't know

I : but you are

Y : which leads me into an impasse

I : and you still feel you've got to you can't be yourself
    what you are really want to be ● what you
    emotionally are

Y : ╫ I don't know what I feel I am

I : I beg your pardon

Y : I was just saying to myself that here I am with you

I : well what do you think you are

Y : I think I am a human being as anybody else ● I used
    to think I am used to think ● couldn't stand being
    one of many ● I told you I couldn't stand maybe
    I should die and the idea of growing old I can't even
    stand it either can't understand the idea total life
    process it is being an ╫ uses a place I felt it
    doesn't mean anything to me ● that's the problem

I : what is the problem

Y : probably trying to ascribe to that ◪ goal of being
        ● recognised

I : (r)(as what)

Y : equally equally as an individual

I : as yourself

Y : as yourself yes

I : as what you are

Y : and not achieving that goal

I : uh uh

Y : that goal where I can

I : naw come one as recognising that goal as being yourself as being what you are do you agree with that

Y : but

I : no hang on would you agree with that

Y : that my goal is to recognise myself as what I am

I : uh is it

Y : why do you say that's the goal

I : you said it

Y : yeah

I : you said that's your problem

Y : the dilemma

I : ah yes I agree but why is it the dilemma because you think recognising yourself as what you are would conflict with what other people might want you to be

Y : yeah that's a good statement as a matter of fact

I : so you are really concerned with what other people think about you

Y : yeah

I : why or even more so why do you think they would have
    a low opinion of you if you were what you are   *   I
    repeat why do you think why do you think other people
    would have a low opinion of you if you were what you
    are which means that you are not now what you are

Y : excuse me if I light a cigarette

I : am I right

Y : yes * in fact *   at a point of my non-understanding

I : you are at a point of non-understanding

Y : 卌

I : sorry

Y : a point that   *   may be subliminal wishful
    acceptance for what I am

I : acceptance for what you are for what you would like
    to be accept for what you think you are

Y : yes what I think I am

I : right well what do you think you are

Y : what do you think I am

I : do you think you are not expressing the feelings that
    you want to express

Y : oh no of course I don't

I : you don't express the feelings you want to express

Y : no yeah I think I've double edged dilemma of existence

I : what's the double edge dilemma

Y : I don't express things that I'm actually • I don't
express when the time comes I don't express I don't
express what's that I don't express what I honestly
care about an individual ⊡ another person and
if I do then I guess I honestly express I am
condemned if I don't I don't why it always seems that

I : why don't you

•

Y : because I look ⊡ I place myself in that other
person's world looking other person's role looking
back at myself

I : and they will reject you

Y : yeah

I : why • I will not reject you anybody anyway
because if that's any consolation

•

Y : well I don't think I would reject you too

I : you'd reject yourself ⊡ why

•

Y : I don't feel I I don't feel I fit into this
structure ⧺ yeah

I : try and break that barrier ⊙ if you can

Y : yeah ◎ ⧺ uhm I'm looking at the pictures

I : which pictures • are you ashamed or something

•

Y : nah

I : no

Y : no I'm not ⊔ ashamed • ooh

I : afraid

Y : afraid

I : you are

Y : yeess

I : what pictures are you seeing

Y : walls walls walls

I : walls in rooms

Y : no fences and gates

I : locked

Y : no keeping me in with them

I : whose them

Y : them   other faces

I : what I'm trying to get you to do ⌷   is to break that
    barrier

Y : yeah

I : to knock down to make a little hole in that fence •   a
    little hole in that wall I've already said I am not
    going to reject you under any circumstances and I can
    easily show you how to break the wall its very much
    better for you if you can do it on your own

Y : I can break down a wall

I : if you want to ⌷   I think you do want to

Y : I don't know maybe I don't want to maybe I

I : do you

Y : thats a problem because I can say   •   you can say
    externally yes I would love to   •   you can say
    and then looking at myself I've been bitten many
    times   •   so I'd rather be aloof

I : no I don't think so   *   you'd rather be aloof
than what   *[]*   people

Y : people yes

I : after that   *   surely not a result of your romantic
idea

Y : I think that is why I have the romantic idea because I
keep myself aloof all the time

I : you'd rather be aloof perhaps than that's a form of
deceit one can be aloof for different reasons one can
try and be aloof as as a form of deceit   *[]*   as an
excuse of not facing up to things so you romanticise
the reasons for your not facing up to things as being
aloof

Y : yeah

I : whereas being aloof perhaps in my case or in certain
cases will be that one only wishes to associate with
people of a certain degree sensitivity or intelligence
or understanding or a desire to be honest one will be
aloof from the lawyers or the people who are most
dishonest or a different form of aloof ones motive
for being aloof is not the same   *   and I'm not
romanticising it I am being quite factual about it

Y : yes I s

I : I suppose you romanticise it

Y : I'll admit thats true I'll romanticise it maybe I
tend to look at all people as dishonest and myself as
totally dishonest more than anyone else

I : well maybe but I think you think you're dishonest

Y : because I have a perception ☐ of what truth is

I : what is truth

Y : that is not because ☐ I've a perception of the way
people should live together which is a romantic
perception a utopian perception ☐ it is totally
un-ideal totally un-wise perception

I : why

Y : because human beings do not live that way

I : what is your perception of why people live that way
•

Y : this is ridiculous

I : this is ridiculous
•

Y : this is ridiculous because this is totally☐futilely☐
short lifetime • uhm a total dissolution of
goal

I : no what I was asking what I was asking is your
perception of why people should live together unless

Y : oh why people should why people should live together

I : according to you its totally romantic a utopian why
people should live together • which is your
concept of truth
•

Y : its my perception of god

I : as well which is what

Y : I think death is truth

I : why is death truth

Y : because you have to live together there's nothing
    else   ◦   (s)(you're all in the ground you're
    all the same)   •   you create all
    different persons death creates different heavens
    and hell ah all these bullshit   •   death is the
    only reality of existence this is being irrelevant
    again

I : no just what you've said   •   do you want to be
    helped

Y : do I want to be yeah a kind of to hear the man I
    want to be its just that I never have been

I : you never have been true

Y : never have been when you say true   .

I : well I know you never have been otherwise you would
    not be here   [c]   here you are now

Y :   [image]   I don't understand that step

I : probably you have you probably never had this sort
    of dialogue with anybody before

Y : of course not you're kidding my
    ◦

I : so because I think   ◦   I think you are are ,
    being quite as honest as you can be   •   sad
    because there's more there's a lot more that you want
    to be lot more you want to try lot more you want to
    know and as I said at the begining I think that you
    are at a point where you know almost where you want
    to go   •   but you will not make that move you'd
    like to make the move that's holding you back is really
    the opinions of other people will think   [c]   about
    you having made that move   .
    ◦

Y : yeah I've seen faces for that one

I : saying what 🔲 doing what 🔲 which faces

Y : mostly my mother my mother exerted I'll have to admit
the basic influence on me

I : she'd be dissapointed 🔲 sad 🔲 unhappy ● is
that it

Y : 𝓗 I guess ● she loves it 🔲 my
brother and myself is the only possessions because
her life is really pretty sad really she she

I : but you think you're moving to a certain standpoint
will do what to her ● changing your perspective
● I guess that implies changing what you are

Y : got to be ● no

I : if you change what you are to become ● something if
you changed what you are now to become what you are in
reality which you feel you are would that disappoint her

Y : yeah

I : why

Y : because

I : you think she'll reject you

Y : no yes

I : yes ● so what is your choice ● you change
and accept the possibility of her rejection which by
the way I must I really am quite sincere 🔲 you can't
believe it 🔲 as a mother if you committed

a ⧓ is unlikely that a mother will ever reject you no matter what you do because she's too much a part of you and you too much a part of her secondly on the alternative if she did reject you she was not worth having as a mother because then her feelings run very shallow deep down they are shallow towards you

Y : yeah

I : that's by the way

Y : I always look at my mother as a person who tries to live all that she did in her in me

I : that may or may not be but thats not what we are talking about we are talking about why you think your mother will reject you

Y : I think thats very relevant to that

I : why what is the connection why

Y : because she was she looks at me at that which she didn't become

I : what did she want you to become

Y : all that she didn't become

I : which is what what did she not become

Y : great someone she wanted to be someone that stood above the crowd someone that made a difference quote unquote made a difference unquote or something

I : OK so

Y : she wanted me too

I : you don't think you'll make a difference

Y : Oh I know I won't

I : why

Y : there's no way I can make a difference to someone else's
individual life

I : you certainly can if you love someone or someone loves you

Y : but so I'm incapable of love

I : you're incapable of love

Y : I know I am I know I am because of because of

I : because of what   •   why get it out ⌷ because
of what

Y : because   •   tire like because I fear I can only
love myself ,   •   something like that

I :   ◁   ♯♩   why can you only love yourself

Y : I could never I don't think I could ever   •   totally
compromise myself to another individual   ⊙   as I
guess I I never loved my family   •   I guess my
family never loved me

I : what do you mean compromise yourself to another
individual

Y : obvious is n't it compromise

I : love

Y : ▨

I : love is perhaps an understanding

Y : an understanding as to what

I : nothing to do its an understanding   •   if there is a
compromise

Y : then

I : if

Y : then I don't understand love

I : no I don't think you do

Y : I don't understand it at all then no

I : that

Y : it at all

I : if there is a compromise in ones relationship as regards
    love then one's not loved even the play last
    indicated that to a certain extent

Y : uoh theres no compromise

I : what he was asking for was a compromise

Y : he was asking for more than a compromise

I : well no

Y : he was asking for an absolvement

I : but

Y : an absolvement

I : no he wasn't actually

Y : oh yeah

I : absolvement you mean an absolvement from what from his

Y : from hurting him

I : from hurting him or from hurting her

Y : her from her to him absolvement of her in him

I : but thats so   so you don't understand love

Y : no I don't understand love at all   in fact   I
    don't her I don't I don't understand the concept
    lets say of

I : do you think you are very selfish

Y : yeah   I know

I : yes and no

Y : I know

I : thats correct yes because you are selfish no because
    you can if you want to be give a lot •   you want or
    not

Y : give a lot

I : give a lot of yourself give a lot of your ⟦c⟧   self
    •

Y : maybe I've never found someone to give that too

I : no you haven't it hurts you but you think you are
    capable of doing it
    •

Y : capable I'd be   •   oh

I : because you've already reached the stage you already
    past the stage of thinking about suicide which means
    you are in a dangerous stage by the way   •   for me
         •   well you haven't committed suicide

Y : oh well its on

I : even if its a thought at the moment

Y : I'm too much of a coward to commit suicide

I : maybe ⟦c⟧   which means you might become •   you
    have choices now why

Y : go on

I : you have two directions in which you'll go
    •

Y : what are the two

I : there are only two

Y :   ⟦⟧   and which does one entail two is just a
    favourite poetic expression

I : no its not there's the right way or the wrong way

Y : the right and the wrong then you have the branch of the
    right and the branch of the wrong

I : well maybe   •   maybe but you're at the point now
    when you choose the right or the wrong

Y : and the wrong will consequently mean what

    •

I : well consequently

Y : either my total compromise in what I cannot be or near
    suicide or

I : that's right

Y : or

    •

I : quite correct quite correct so you know that

Y : or a total yeah

I : or a total

Y : or a total unhappiness

I : correct

    •

Y : or the right decision will make me either   ⊘   happy
    and a   ⊡   satisfied individual in relation to
    others

I : and yourself

Y : and myself let me

I : not necessarily but yes   •   right so you

Y : the bathroom

I : sorry

Y : in the bathroom   ⚐ → ♪

I :   _sss_ (T)   Hi sandy is senn there • I got a call about an arrangement can we make it about 11 tomorrow • right so can he leave a message either to make it earlier or about five six in the afternoon • what time can he come as I'm playing some tennis tomorrow morning he said he would try and make it tomorrow morning

Y : yeah yeah

I : ask him to give me a ring as to what time he can come tomorrow morning if its between twelve and twelve thirty that's fine super we'll be seeing one another over the weekend • super • yeah' OK yeah not enough work done but OK yeah I've seen a few plays • maybe come to lunch Sunday • Ok we'll speak tomorrow OK bye sandy bye _sss_ (T) _rep._ so you know actually in fact

Y : yeah

I : so you know you know you have to make a choice

Y : choices what

I : yea but the choice in your case is far more profound and far more important

Y : it depends with what the importance is

I : you

Y : me

I : yes

Y : I to myself

I : well you can either

Y : well the

I : ⌠·· well you can either

Y : ⌡·· well the importance of what to the whole

I : you reckon

Y : the whole is itself but myself is only you of course

I : it it is totally insignificant you can of course commit
suicide and end it if you want to

Y : yeah

I : it's one of the choices it will make no real difference
to choose the wrong direction at the moment because

Y : yeah I know

I : because physical suicide doesn't matter you will have
committed personal moral [◌] real suicide and it
anything will be all the more difficult for you to
backtrack you might backtrack but I doubt it ◦
backtrack and switch · to the right path [◌].
backtrack means in the sense that you well have already
walked say ten yards 10 million yards two yards 2000
kilometers and you'll have to [◌] you don't have to
physically turn around you'll have to acknowledge
that that was the wrong path path and start on the
right one ◦ acknowledge to yourself which may
mean acknowledging to other people but it may mean its
more difficult

Y : well I know it well with other people

I : what you do happens to set you on the wrong path being
wrong is dishonest you are not you ◦ you're not what
you want to be [◌] you're not what you want to do
tell me if I'm wrong

Y : you're not wrong   in that way

I : its just I'm not wrong you're not wrong I know you are
    wrong you know you are wrong

Y : ⧻

I : sorry

Y : thats just what I'm trying to say

I : but you know what you should do

Y : the question is   ▱   as you have said many times
    already why don't I go for the right path

I : right I I can change in a flash

Y : now I don't understand what makes it so difficult for
    me

I : well I know what makes it so difficult for you
    pain

Y : you're in a state of reflection I'm in a state of
    intuitive   reflection

I : yes yea quite so and I'm and I'm trying to bring your
    intuitive reflection up to a conscious level
    because I think that will help you   so a lot
    of things you've said now have not been reflected have
    come come up   they have not been conscious or
    if they have come up and I try to pinpoint on them
    sometimes I have some I haven't

Y : yes

I : and when I say to you once that you have passed a
    barrier is what I'm trying to say for you consciously
    to pass the barrier   subconscious and thats
    the conflict of course because you over there

Y : to attain the unity of the subconscious with the
conscious

I : well well maybe but

Y : is that possible   •   is that possible to attain   •
for an iceberg to attain its

I : yea I agree its a good question   •   you have two ways
of doing it either non verbally or verbally either by
physical action or

Y : well I can attain to get the reality right

I : well yes you can but thats not what I'm talking about

Y : yeah I know so maybe its a reflexive thing   .

I : what I am saying is you've changed your perspective
you already over there subconsciously   •   nine
tenths of the iceberg to use your and its causing
you a lot of unhappiness and has been for a long
time   •   I'm trying to shift you across to
that point trying to get you to shift yourself   •   if
you want to

Y : yes

I : which you do   •   alternatively to ask for me
to help you

Y : no I don't think thats proper ah

I : too foolish to ask then

Y : yeah because probably I'd do the same thing again

I : yea sure

Y :   •   strange that at the point that   •   I
can ask for help

I : you do its fairly easy to ask for help

Y :   yes extreemly easy but at the point where
you want to ask for help you think why should I ask for
help why which gets back to the word the absurd level why
would you be interested

I :

Y : both to the   that I'm projecting untruth in you which is
in me

I : thats correct and I'm wondering if

Y : I believe you I'm sorry I'm sorry sorry

I : it makes no difference if you believe me or not whatever
my motives or whatever it is that is an entirely different
question

Y : yes true I've known that for a long time now

I : what

Y : your sincerity

I : how

Y : I can deduce

I : how

Y : you just feel it I'm I don't know I can't explain it in
words your sincerity   which is the dilemma of language
   I can I can feel it I can easily feel it
oh this is a question a question that you wouldn't the
perfect question of why you wouldn't prove it the perfect
instances that you have

I : I wouldn't do what

Y : you have you not have posed the question of why as a a
perfect instance instance instances that you have no
one has ever posed why in the position you have   uhm

I : you see

Y : uhm

I : sorry

Y : can't you see you still that genuine   *   it means
    a lot

I : its very small

Y : well thats what the iceberg is the one one tenth is
    all that you see

I : certainly I see but I see the nine tenths   *   I also
    see the one tenth

Y : of my iceberg

I : take a look

Y : why

I : take off the mask and ask for   ♯♯

Y : mask what mask do you take off

I : the one that you've put on

Y :   ▲   you just can't   ▲   is it the right one
    or is there

I : you will not know until you take it off

Y : or is there many of them

I : there may be there may well be very many of them but
    until you take it off the one that is there

Y : do you peel

I : I think you actually want to take it off

Y : I think you're actually right

I : so lets give how to see to take it off

Y : how to take yes how to take it off   as in
    how did you ask help or

I : well the two go hand in hand how to help and how to
    take off the mask

Y : how

I : how to help how to take off the mask but

Y : the one man dilemma how

I : maybe maybe I don't think its the dilemma of all men
    because I think very few people get to the point where
    they want to be honest

Y : hmm

I : and be themselves

Y : artisan

I : sorry

Y : artisan

I : artisan

Y : artisan the art

I : maybe

Y : the how the how

I : you don't want to be you are in a way ⌐⊘ already

Y : in a way

I : you know that one sees that one recognises that I see

Y : I

I : that one sees

Y : one of the glasses is empty now

I : more wine

Y : time yes

I : yes

Y : wine is not necessary

I : tell you about human existence that is why one goes on despite the shocks we manage to survive to survive

Y : despite all this this paper bullshit

I : whats that

Y : do you believe the Falklands exist

I : the Falklands Island

Y : yes

I : of course they exist

Y : why do they exist

I : why do they exist

Y : yeah

I : what do you mean why do they exist

Y : in what way do they exist to you

I : because they are there because there's suffering the because there are people there because they are stuck there because they ⌐⊘ they just exist

Y : they

I : they have not touched me deep inside yet one photograph actually of an Argentinian which

Y : yeah   of course it would touch you but this this
     does not touch you

I : it's a newspaper article a waste of time   •   what
     do you think why do you not ask for help

Y : yes why am I afraid   •   that someone else would know
     more of me than me

I : well I know more of you

Y : thats an omission   •   how long how long its been
     thats thats   •   dunno something

I : on your part

Y : yeah on my part yeah

I : So you think I know more about you than you do

Y : in relation

I : in relation to what

Y : in relation   •   uhm   uhm I don't know uhm   ⊘   in
     relation as to what I am about

I : as to what you are

Y : sure pure   ⊘   with out   •   you even more than
     •   aider moi

I : is it fear

Y : yeah its fear you ask if it's fear

I : what fear is it

Y : possibly a percentage of pride possibly a greater
     percentage of fear

I : is that so

Y : hmm

I : you think so

Y : I'd surprise you

I : I've already said I will not reject you what I think is
    that you reject yourself

Y : what if I reject myself in front of you would that
    be a total rejection

I : how can you reject yourself in front of me

Y : yes but   ☉   I mean reject   ✎   how would you
    reject ⬚ someone   ✎   who you   ✎   face
    of   ✎   show it to

I : thats virtually incognito

Y : thats a rejection of whom

I : well the concept of rejection could only come into
    it if there was a dislike of it the mask

Y : by the way you ask

I : the only reason why

Y : the mask would fall ⬚ off I'd show it to you

I : once the mask fell off I don't think it can be put on
    at least

Y : through what through you

I : through nothing

Y : through nothing

I : what is underneath the mask

Y : how do you know what is underneath the mask

I : well I can see for the last 20 odd minutes as long
as you think I am immobile 🔲 so I know its there

Y : see the mask put off and then put on again

I : whether I see the mask off or on when its on

Y : its just that I see in the mirror the mask on

I : no no its just that   •   you scared

Y : yeah •   but I still see the mask on   •   I guess
that's the question I'm pardon on   ⊙   why do we
have a mask in the first place

I : to hide our true emotions to hide where we are 🔲
society pressures family millions of reasons 🔲 to
hide isn't that the mask

Y : to hide   •   draw a smile or draw a flower   •   I'll
draw a flower   ⊛   jesus   🔲   christ

    •

I : sorry your eyes beginning to eyes beginning to see

Y : yes

I : true black

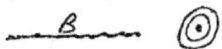

Y : no you know these masks are just eyes just

I : masks are just eyes

Y : eyeslip for a cover for them I can't see a cover on them

I : sorry

Y : I can't see a cover on them the eyeslips

I : but they are not

Y : ₤₸

I : its what you are fearing

Y : its evasive

I : why can't   •   thats a fear not a crime crime   • is
     not going to make you evasive how do you make it over

Y : yeah probably go to hell I'm saying no point in it
     what I'm saying I think excuse me I think therefore
     I am I think

    •

I : hmm

Y : criticise the point if you can

I : ▼

Y : and still I can't grasp

I : grasp what

    •

Y : the fact that its being caused   🔲   the fact that.
     its

I : pride is a very minor point it was an excuse

Y : yeah thats a very good point

I : so you realsie that it was an excuse   •   it was not
     a false excuse there was a certain degree it may have
     been a false excuse in that you pushed the pride which was
     not there   (•)   you have to make your steps

    •

Y : which steps step   go up and down

I : no no

Y : ah

I : well yes they do no they don't go down well they can go
     down but its two different paths two alternatives you
     can go down or you can go up you can remain static as
     well if you want to

Y : ⌠·· you want

I : ⌡·· you want (r)(sorry)

Y : ⎰ --well walk by
I : ⎱ ··why you can walk straight on you can walk straight
      on or over   •   the edge or you can walk up you want to
      walk up

      •

Y : thats a hard thing to say in the last whole half hour
      or so I've been grasping to say something but

I : what

      •

Y : I'm trying to say something but   •   its nothing

I : well if its nothing say it

Y : its nothing I've simple and to go but   •   nothing
      is ever the same .

I : anyway you know what you want to say

Y : in a way   kinda way the admission that I can't
      live without another person aaghgh

I : is that what you want to say

Y : thats not the worst said but aaghgh its that   true ah

I : by and large yes I think its true in your case anybody
      needs something somebody else in a way

Y : and you are saying that includes me

I : you need somebody I know you do

Y : hmm

I : I think I know what you need   I think you know what
      you need   •   is that what you have been trying to
      say you you can't live with someone else

Y : ha

I : is that just part

Y : I can't be me

I : no I think thats just part of it * thats all of it
    *   go on

*

Y : a corner a cat in the wall

*

I : you feel you are in a corner at the moment * can't
    say

Y : no

I : you don't

Y : no you don't * but its a corner of sorts its not
    what you'd expect

I : whats the one you'd expect

Y : the corner that I was *⃗ thinking of * is that
    right is that right the corner that of the * the
    projection of yourself that others see

I ; well a possible corner you might feel in is that you
    know that firstly that I know and secondly that * is
    that

Y : is that a gross dilemma that I am in ▲ that I'm in
    a corner that I know * that I know that someone
    else knows that what I do know what I don't choose to know

I : what you don't choose to know

Y : what I don't choose to know * it means that I don't
    choose to know * exists an answer * I'll
    take a wall

I : quite correct and also the fact is that the corner
    you know that whatever you might want to say now is
          *   you can't * turn around and say

something false   ●   or you can if you want to but it
will cut no ice so you're you're in a corner

Y : I can say irrelevancies yes

I : it will cut no ice

Y : yeah

I : so you're in a corner now in the sense that you can't

Y : you say you say false or you say true

I : you can you can say false and I will know its false I
mean you can take that as an extra if you want to but
as far as the reality the many instances so you either
come out or you don't there are no more exits just   walls
●

Y : my brother and mice I still can do it

I : oh no you can't

Y : I could because I just

I : that would be the wrong path if you want ◙ you could of course

Y : yeah yeah I yeah   ●   I guess that explains a little
portion of my character that I would even think that
    ●   naw its less than think

I : I think you may have gone beyond the stage of fearing
    ●   but but I sense that
●

Y : No I'm afraid of fear

I : because you are not necessary   ●   we are talking
behind the words that we are talking to one another
there's an understanding   ●   at least I think you
accept there's something whatever it is many things
    ●   I think you're being more honest now   ●   come
out come out with what you really want to say and do or
feel   ●   or not to

Y : not to I turn I'd turn everybody against me

I : every single day of your life you have that option to
turn against what is reality what is the truth what
is the light

Y :   can I ask what is reality

I : well you know in a way

Y : ―··I know at least

I : ―·· what is reality

Y : when you face the wall there is light

I : thats right who knows what reality is you have to keep
moving towards the light you can face the wall and you'll
not move you may move backwards

Y : you'll walk

I : you'll crawl and this is not in symbolic reprsentation
of movement   you want to walk

Y : you crawl before you walk

I : you want to crawl

Y : keep crawling

I : its immaterial if you want to fly to walk or what do you
you all come to it depends depends after

Y : its a stage

I : no it depends after you initial step

Y : what that you want to walk or stage just to clarify
it for me

I : make it or not

Y : make what you say make up an answer

I : make it or not

Y : oh   *⊿*   sorry

I : the initial step   ⊙   you want or you don't want to

Y : is that a yes or no question

I : yes

Y : hm

I : it is

Y : I have done to yet   •   I have to answer yes   •   I have answered .

I : then translate that into action

Y : action as what

I : action as words action as movement action as thought

Y : I think I could think

I : tell us your thoughts   •   either verbally or non-verbally   •   you are half way there

⊙

Y :   ▩   its easy to its easy to

I : put into action

Y :   ▽   action is ⊙ what is it like action fear

I : what an idea of trying   •   once you make the right action in either direction   •   but you've got to make the action

Y : I can't   •   I can't but I can diminish my

my previous point or that I can achieve ⊚ ⊔ I can't

I : come on

Y : for a point a wall no anyone can translate into action ready or not ready

I : ready or not ready ● I feel a bit hard

Y : pardon

I : I feel as if I'm being a bit hard on you

Y : you couldn't be

I : you're alone make the stage

Y : pardon

I : close just a bit

Y : no

I : a corner

Y : a corner

I : then do it

Y : ▲ (s) (immense room)

I : make it small

Y : a corner I'd do it ⊙ I'll never do it

I : sorry

Y : I'll never

I : its not so immense when you think talk about it its very small ⊙ ↳ → ● you might have something

Y : pardon

I : maybe you learn ⊚ are you in pain

Y : yeah

I : you are

Y : not nausea   ●   escape from it   ●   the tin
    in my soul

I : you can't escape from pain

○

Y : pardon

I : you're close

Y : then the admission that I need help

I : if you want to   ●   warmth

Y : if I need help then what am I   ●   its cold its
    terribly cold in the corner

○

I : do you want ▱ break the wall

   ●

Y : do you tolerate these questions   ●   I've
    heard of suicide or   ●   (r)(success)   ●   to
    be   extreme   ●   in fact   ●   you can help
    me   ●   yeah   ●   what am I

   ●

I : listen to it   ○   yes or no
○

Y : yes

I : are you sure

Y : you asked yes or no yeah thats what I mean yes

I : thats it

Y : thats what I mean

I : what do you mean

hey you ! out there in the cold

getting lonely , getting old , can you feel me

I : where are you

Y : over here I can't make you can't   help

hey you ! standing in the aisles

with itchy feet and fading smiles can you feel me

hey you ! don't help them to bury the light

don't give up without a fight

hey you ! with your ear against the wall

waiting for someone to call out would you touch me

hey you ! would you help me to carry the stone

Open your heart I'm coming home

But it was only fantasy

the wall was too high as you can see

no matter how he tried he could not break free

and the worms ate into his brain

hey you ! out there on the road

doing what you're told can you help me

hey you ! out there beyond the wall

breaking bottles in the hall can you help me

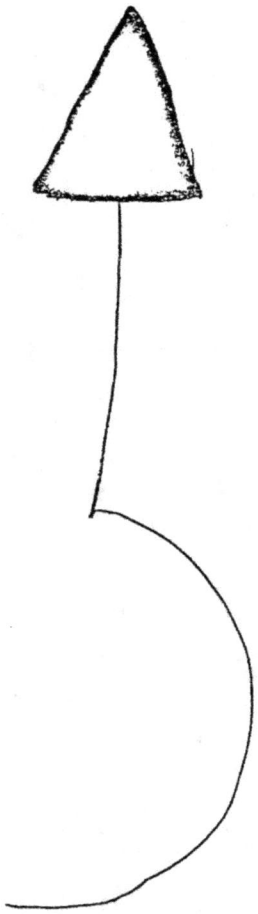

Afterword

The first publication had no pagination, as the page numbers interfered with the structure – a little like an artist's signature may interfere with the painting. I have been persuaded by the publishers to have page numbers and these are top right as un-intrusive as possible while still accepting the need for pagination. Hopefully one day soon the technical wizards will allow pagination to be cloaked and to be switched on or off, made visible only when required.

orde, Oxford, June 2014.

Note by the Publisher 2013

Mæg ic be me sylfum	I can make a true song
soðgied wrecan,	about me myself,

The Seafarer, date unknown.(Approximate translation of the old English)

Song, established in 2013 is an imprint of a new publication house, a division of Song of the Wild Swan Ltd.

It publishes any writings from anyone who has a song.

Song also participates in the BEL (Barter Exchange Levy) Price System.

List of Selected Works by orde

Song, November 2013
Areas of classification may overlap

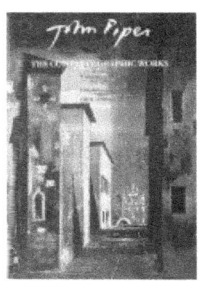

Books

1   *John Piper – The Complete Graphic Works: A
     Catalogue Raisonné 1923-1983.* Compiled and
     edited by Orde Levinson. Faber & Faber,
     1988.

2   *I Was Lonelyness: The Complete Graphic Works
     of John Muafangejo 1968-1987.* Struik
     Winchester, 1992. Foreword by Archbishop
     Desmond Tutu. Contributing essays from:
     Olga Levinson (The Life and Art of John
     Muafangejo); Edward Lucie-Smith (John
     Muafangejo); Pat Gilmour (On Not Being a
     Political Artist); Orde Levinson (John
     Muafangejo, Cubism and Traditional African

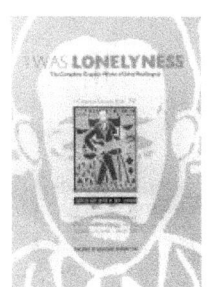

     Art); Olga Levinson (The Historical
     Development of Art in Namibia) and Steven
     Sack (The Rorke's Drift Art and Craft
     Centre) and all Muafangejo's Interviews,
     Statements and published conversations.

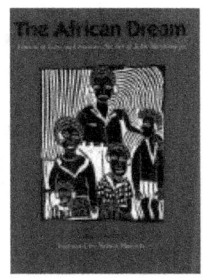

3   *The African Dream – Visions of Love and
     Sorrow. The Art Of John Muafangejo.* Thames
     and Hudson, 1993. Foreword by Nelson
     Mandela.

4   *Quality and Experiment. The Prints of John
     Piper – A Catalogue Raisonné.* Lund
     Humphries, 1996.

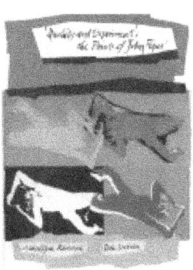

5   *The Prints of John Piper – A Catalogue Raisonné
     1921-1991.* Lund Humphries, 2010.
     Contributing essays Introduction (Orde
     Levinson); Experiment and Quality (Orde
     Levinson); Subject and Technique in Piper's
     Printmaking (David Fraser Jenkins); Working
     with Printers (John Piper).

6   *Hitting the Nail on the Head – The Complete Written Works of John Piper 1913-1992.* An estimated three volumes with contributing essays by various authors (tba). Scheduled for publication 2014/5.

7   *Delights and Aphorisms, selected writings of John Piper.* Scheduled for publication 2014-5.

8   *Daniel Henry Kahnweiler: A bibliography.* Scheduled for publication 2014.

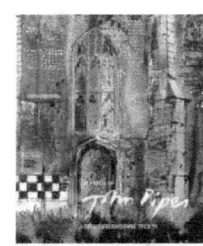

9   *The Life and Work of Daniel Henry Kahnweiler: A critical evaluation.* Originally part of the D. Phil. Study at Magdalen College, Oxford University. Scheduled for publication 2015.

10   *The Complete Writings of Daniel Henry Kahnweiler.* Three volumes. Scheduled for publication 2015-6.

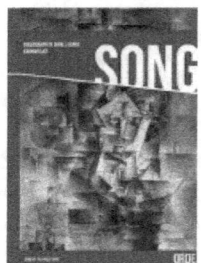

Conversations and interviews

11   *orde's Conversations with Henry Moore.* Henry Moore talks about influences, the artists he likes, his work and life in general. Available as eBook 2013 Book published by Song 2014

12   *Orde's Conversations with Richard Sorabji (videoed)* in progress,. Richard Sorabji in thought and in person is brought to us in a unique experiment where orde has selected friends from each decade to converse with him. Completed to date are Louis Hynes (age 10); Laurence Hutton-Smith (age 20); Richard Kuziara (age 37); Lisa Hammond-Marty (age 40-50); Jeremy Rowe (age 50-58); Marianne Talbot (age 58--68) Joanna Foster (age 68-80). Available as video, eBook and book. Scheduled publication 2015.

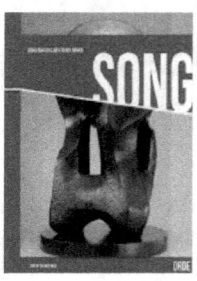

13   *Talking to Solly Irwin (videoed)* Schedule publication as eBook and book 2014-5,

Films

14   *Essences.* Independent production
produced by orde under the inspiration of
Straub and Huillet. A contemplative
mood piece starring Richard E. Grant
and Kiki Savejan
Director/script/editor: orde
Cast: Richard E Grant, Kiki Savejan
Running Time: 40 minutes/colour
Date Completed: 1983
(Image: Scene Shot from Essences by orde.)

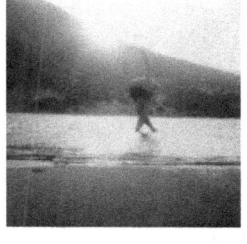

15   *Ÿ*
Director/script/editor: orde
Cast: Richard E Grant
Running time:16 minutes/colour
Date Completed: c.1987.

Film scripts

16   *The Judgment of Shylock.* In progress.

In fermentation/digestion

17   *The Inventors dilemma.* A novel?
18   *Five Fingers are not the same.* A novel?
19   *Turquoise.* A love story.
20   *The Weather of myself.* A philosophical book/diary.
21   *The Human Tragedy.* A true story, novel/poem?

Music

22   *I am here thank you please, a musical
composition.* Contains an introduction on
classical and romantic by orde.
Available 2014 as eBook and book (published
by Song.

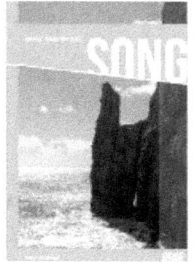

23   *Le Bordel Philosophique.* A musical composition
with 5 contemporary composers (George
Barton, Sam Fernando, Cheryl Francis-Hoad, Simon Roth, Jaime
Wolfson). A composition based on a poem, which is based on a
painting to reach a musical gesamtkunstwerk for our era.
Scheduled for completion 2014.

Plays

24   *Forcible Love.* A play based on the life of John
        Muafangejo.

25   *Forcible Love (NTN version).* A musical on the
        life of John Muafangejo - premiered at the
        National Theatre, Windhoek, Namibia for the
        Independence Celebrations. Includes reviews.
        Available 2014 as eBook and book (published
        by Song)

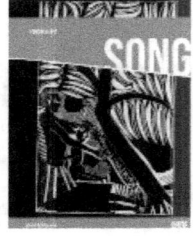

26   *The Rialto Dialogues.* Described as a
        revolutionary work about the Merchant of
        Venice by William Shakespeare. It includes the
        entire work uncut but introduces 4 new
        characters to open a meaning and channel to
        one of Shakespeare's greatest plays.
        Available 2014 as eBook and book (published
        by Song)

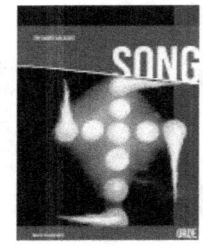

27   *Shylock the Magnificent.* A play 13 years after
        the Trial Scene of the Merchant of Venice by Shakespeare.
        Available 2014 as eBook and book (published by Song)
        See also The Soul's Heritage under poems.

Poems

28   *Miscellaneous poems.* Short poems found over
        the years.
        Available 2014 as eBook and book.

29   *The Love song of D. Adolph Hitler.* In progress.

30   *Der Tod Des Miguel.* In progress

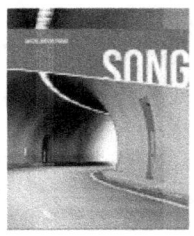

31   *Les Dem.* About Picasso's painting *Les Demoiselles D'Avignon*,
        includes essay on *Les Dem* by Professor Andrew Laird.
        Available 2014 as eBook and book (published by Song).

32   *Ndilapa Nkosi.* A lyrical comedy, first part of *The Soul's Heritage*, a
        trilogy, a landmark work described by Samuel Beckett as a
        'moving feat'. Includes reviews and responses from various persons
        including Beckett.

Available 2014 as eBook and book (published by Song).

33 *Antomat Diplony of the Orb.* An epic comedy, in progress, second part of The Soul's Heritage, a trilogy.

34 *The Argonauta Vineyard.* A tragic comedy, in progress, third part of The Soul's Heritage, a trilogy.

35 *Parlez à Voir.*
Available 2014 as eBook and book (published by Song).

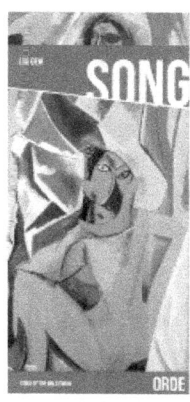

36 *Flying strongly on one wing.*
Available 2014 as eBook and book (published by Song).

37 *Snowflakes and Ashes.*
Available 2014 as eBook and book (published by Song).

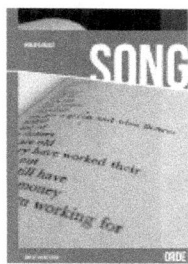

Reviews and articles

38 A number of articles and reviews exist and are being collated.

39 *Art, An Adaptive Function?*
Encyclopaedia of Evolution Mark Pagel (Editor-in-Chief), Oxford University Press, 2002. (365 articles from 330 different authors).

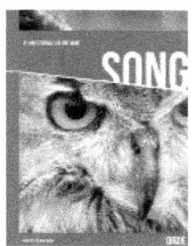

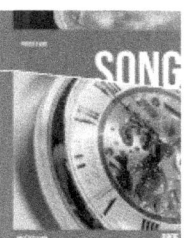

Visual works

Drawings, paintings, photography, prints. sculptures
Please see www.orde.info